PRAISE & WORSHIP
DRUMMING
A GUIDE TO PLAYING IN CHURCH

by
CARY NASATIR

PLAYBACK+
Speed • Pitch • Balance • Loop

To access audio visit:
www.halleonard.com/mylibrary

3324-9471-0285-5587

ISBN 978-0-634-08389-1

HAL•LEONARD®

Visit Hal Leonard Online at
www.halleonard.com

Contact Us:
Hal Leonard
7777 West Bluemound Road
Milwaukee, WI 53213
Email: info@halleonard.com

In Europe, contact:
Hal Leonard Europe Limited
42 Wigmore Street
Marylebone, London, W1U 2RN
Email: info@halleonardeurope.com

In Australia contact:
Hal Leonard Australia Pty. Ltd.
4 Lentara Court
Cheltenham, Victoria, 3192 Australia
Email: info@halleonard.com.au

DEDICATION

This book is dedicated to the memory of Tom Patten, a dynamic leader, percussionist, and inspirational friend who was taken too early.

ACKNOWLEDGMENTS

I would like to thank my wife Jan for her love, her editing prowess, and her encouragement on this project; my son Travis for his Finale™ help; my students, Pauline Wong, for her input and music resources, and Fanny Nudo the Editing Queen; Patrick Waller; Roy Burns; Dom Famularo; Mike Hoff; Neil Larrivee; Jim Catalano; and my students who helped field-test the material in this book. I would also like to thank the good folks at Vic Firth, Aquarian, Sabian, Ludwig, and Rhythm Tech for their support and help with all things that are percussion.

The accompanying audio was recorded at Studio Bard in Portland, Oregon.

Table of Contents

INTRODUCTION

Playing in church requires the drummer or percussionist to know many different styles of secular music—from a simple country rock beat, to a waltz, or a calypso rhythm. Whether you are a worship leader or a drummer (or both!), I hope you will find this book to be a useful resource, as I have included the titles of popular praise songs that use the patterns in this book. You will find that the patterns are set up in logical musical phrases that will help you in "real world" playing situations. The drummer is encouraged to experiment with the patterns and fills on the following pages and adapt them to his or her personal playing style, as well as that of the musical group. For clarity, all references to sticking, hands, and feet are from the perspective of a right-handed drummer. If you are left-handed, simply reverse the sticking suggestions.

The secret to playing in a worship band is to use these popular rhythms in a *conservative* manner so that the Word does not get covered up by the drumming. Although percussion is an important element of the worship team, ultimately it is the music, the spirit, and the message that must clearly shine through to the congregation.

Enjoy!

how to use this book

The patterns in this book are set up to give the drummer not only some rhythms to work with but also variations and rhythmic solo breaks called "fills." The two- and four-measure patterns that follow each section will help the drummer attain musicality and phrasing in his or her approach to percussion.

Like pop music, the music used in praise and worship music is built in combinations of two- , four- , and eight-measure phrases. It is important to be aware that *some* variation to the rhythm needs to occur on the fourth and eighth measures. At times the music may need only a single note added on the bass drum; at other times something less subtle may be called for. When the music opens up from a verse to the chorus or bridge, a fill helps with the transition of the tune and elevates the mood of the song. It is good drumming not only to use a fill, but also to change the *color* of your sound. This change can be accomplished by moving from the closed hi-hat, for instance, to the ride cymbal. If you are using a cross stick, get off the rim and strike the drumhead directly. If you are using brushes, switch to sticks. If you are already playing on the ride cymbal, move up to the bell of the cymbal, etc. When you return to the verse, you may want to change back to your original sound. Taste should prevail. It does not help the music if you throw every rhythm lick you know into one measure. If you clutter up your drumming with too many licks, you run the risk of clashing with the bass, the lead instrument, the vocal, and at times, a second percussionist. Listen to well-produced recordings of your favorite musical groups and start to take note of the changes occurring at the places that I have mentioned.

The pages that follow were derived from lessons with my private students and ensembles. What works well is to play a rhythm pattern many times until you feel comfortable with it at different speeds. Start slowly and count out loud. If a pattern is tricky for you, try playing with the hands *only* first, and add the foot or feet later. For some patterns, it may feel better for you to do the opposite by starting with the feet. The two- and four-measure combinations I offer here are only examples of the form. You are encouraged to play any pattern for three measures and add your own fill or variation on the fourth measure. Do the same thing to create eight-measure patterns as well.

Be aware that placing a one-measure fill on an odd measure, like the first or third, can be awkward for the band and should therefore usually be avoided. Likewise, switching patterns or colors mid-phrase is equally startling. If, for instance, I start an eighth-note pattern on the closed hi-hat and realize the ride cymbal would sound better, experience has taught me to say, "No. I'm stuck with it for at least eight measures" (or until the verse changes to make that switch). Chances are that as much as you may not have liked the sound or pattern, it would sound worse and unmusical to switch gears in the middle of a phrase. One more thing: no matter whose fault it *really* is, when the band is rushing or dragging, invariably the drummer will be blamed! Don't rush or drag—especially when playing fills.

GLOSSARY

Accent (>): Emphasis placed on a note or beat by playing louder.

Bridge, Chorus: The "B" section of a piece of music in AABA or ABA form. The intensity usually changes at this point, and sometimes the key or mode changes as well.

Cross Stick (also known as a *rim click, rim knock,* or *butt tap*): The left stick is positioned to be laid across the snare drum. The tip is left on the drumhead, while the butt of the stick hits the opposite rim to make a *pop* sound.

Fill or Break: Short solo lasting under four counts (generally) that helps the music move along. These are especially useful in a transition to a different phrase or section of the song. Customarily, these breaks come on count *three* or *four.*

Laid Back: Playing on the back side of the beat without dragging.

Ride Pattern: Rhythm foundation played on cymbal or hi-hat.

Rute: A bundled set of wooden dowels. They are a bit louder than brushes and have the control of a stick at a lower volume.

Syncopation: Rhythmic device that accents the weak beat instead of the strong beat.

Time Signature: Composer's sign at the beginning of the music (or where a change may occur within the music) expressed as a fraction. The top number tells you how many beats there are in the measure, while the bottom number tells you the type of note that will receive one beat. For example, 4/4 (also known as *common* time and sometimes indicated with a "C") means that there are four beats to the measure (the top number), and each quarter note (bottom number) receives one beat. The beats are counted as "one, two, three, etc." 6/8 means there are *six* beats to the measure, and every *eighth* note receives one beat or numbered count.

Verse: The "A" section of a piece of music in ABA form.

Lesson 1 • the basics
parts of the drumset

Ride Cymbal Tom Toms Crash Cymbal Hi-Hat Snare Drum Floor Tom Bass Drum

stick technique

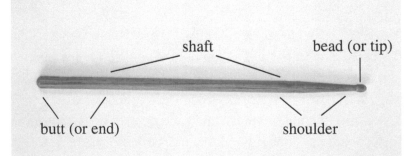

shaft bead (or tip) butt (or end) shoulder

Holding the sticks may seem pretty basic, but there are subtleties that can make or break your technique. There are two basic ways to hold drum sticks: the *matched grip* and the *traditional grip*.

The Matched Grip

This is perhaps the easier of the two most widely used grips. The matched grip is so named because both hands hold the sticks in the same manner. This is also a great grip for left-hand players who play on a right-handed/right-footed drum set.

1. Pick up a stick at about the lower third (at the butt end) with the first finger and thumb. The stick should be held between the first and second knuckle joint of the first finger. The first finger may, but doesn't have to, touch the thumb.
2. Gently wrap the remaining fingers around the stick and lightly pull the stick towards the palm.
3. In most cases, the stick will be balanced when you extend the end about an inch or so just beyond the palm where your wrist creases are.
4. Turn the palms down towards the floor with the thumbs facing each other, and you will have a grip that will serve you well. You may find that your thumbs rotate up a bit as you play on cymbals. This is fine.
5. Holding the sticks tightly limits your technique and makes it difficult to control your volume. Use a relaxed up and down motion of the wrists and avoid the use of the arms. Drum rolls are better achieved by keeping the first finger and thumb in place while *slightly* removing the last three fingers off of the stick.

The Traditional Grip

This older grip lends itself to good volume control with no loss in power. Additionally, some players find that brush technique is easier and smoother with this grip.

1. The right hand remains the same as the matched grip described above.
2. With the left hand, form a karate chop.
3. Place the butt end of the stick into the fleshy webbing of the left thumb. Leave about two inches of the stick extended beyond this point.
4. Place the first two fingers on top of the stick, with the remaining two fingers below the stick. The stick should rest on top of the ring finger between the first and second knuckle joints.
5. Gently pull the fingers and stick towards the palm. The wrist should be in a vertical position. This will allow the wrist to rotate for the basic up and down stroke (avoid motion in the arm). Relax the fingers. It is not necessary for the ring finger and pinky to touch the palm. At times, a little pinch or downward pressure from the first finger and thumb is all that is needed to control the stick.

pedal technique

Bass Drum

There are two basic approaches to playing the bass drum pedal: *heel down* and *heel up*. In the *heel down* position, the player's right foot is placed squarely on the pedal and, while the heel remains on the footboard, the ankle acts as a pivot point. The ankle propels the weight of the foot forward to the pedal—not unlike what the wrist does for stick technique. One advantage to this method is that volume seems to be easily controllable.

In the *heel up* position, the ball of the foot rests on the top half of the pedal. This technique is not unlike tap dancing and uses the lighter front part of the foot to transfer energy to the pedal. Quick repetitions on the bass drum seem easily executed with this method. Either technique is preferable to lifting the foot entirely off the pedal and dropping the weight of the leg onto the footboard of the pedal. This leg lift technique makes volume control very difficult, is hard on pedal straps and chains, and wears out drum heads quickly.

With any pedal technique, the height at which the player is seated is important for comfort, speed, and control. This is why an adjustable throne is so important. If one sits too low, depending on one's height, the leg is bent in such a way that it inhibits the ankle from working well. Bending the leg at the knee too much changes the center of gravity and makes the foot feel heavy and sluggish on the pedal. Sitting higher and straightening the leg a bit takes pressure off the foot and frees up the ankle, resulting in better control and speed. Like adding salt and pepper to food, go easy with height adjustments until you find the height that's right for you.

Heel Down

Heel Up

Hi-Hat

Technique on this instrument is a mixed bag. Someone who, for instance, plays heel down on the bass drum pedal, may play heel *up* on the hi-hat. Lifting the left foot entirely off of the pedal may be necessary sometimes when the hi-hat cymbals need to "cut" through the music ensemble. One technique not used on the bass drum, but perfectly normal for the hi-hat, would be to rock the foot forward and back on the foot board. In this method, the left foot pivots from the ankle throwing the energy of the foot forward towards the toes while lifting the heel up. This method propels the cymbals shut, producing a powerful "chick" sound that other instrumentalists listen for when playing swing or shuffle rhythms, for instance.

When playing on a closed hi-hat, it is a good practice to keep the heel up with pressure from the toes on the footboard. This gives the player the tightest and therefore cleanest sound for eighth- and sixteenth-note rhythm patterns.

NOTATIONAL key

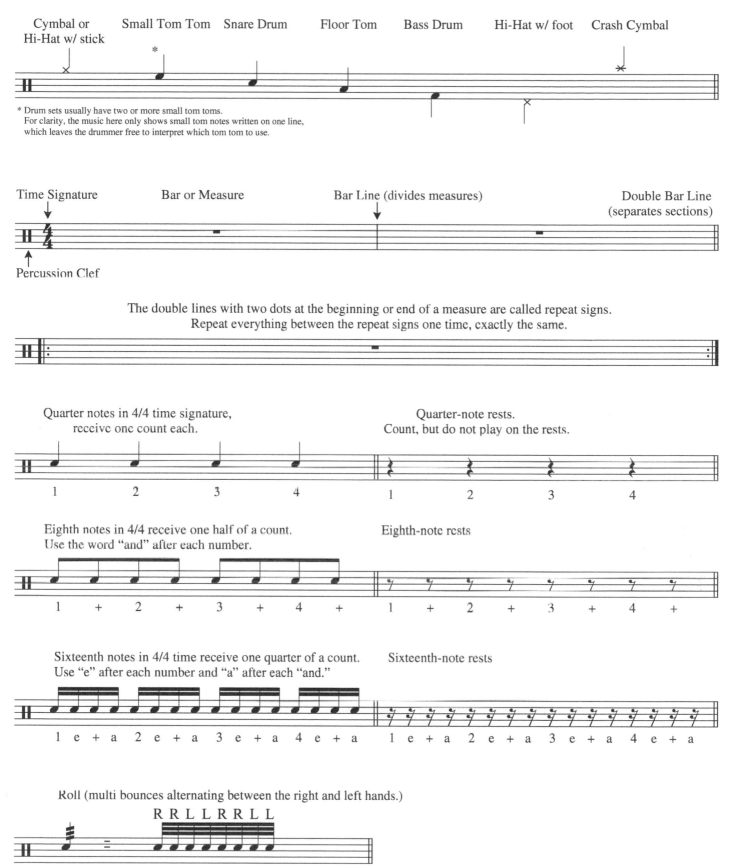

Cymbal or Hi-Hat w/ stick | Small Tom Tom | Snare Drum | Floor Tom | Bass Drum | Hi-Hat w/ foot | Crash Cymbal

* Drum sets usually have two or more small tom toms.
  For clarity, the music here only shows small tom notes written on one line,
  which leaves the drummer free to interpret which tom tom to use.

Time Signature | Bar or Measure | Bar Line (divides measures) | Double Bar Line (separates sections)

Percussion Clef

The double lines with two dots at the beginning or end of a measure are called repeat signs.
Repeat everything between the repeat signs one time, exactly the same.

Quarter notes in 4/4 time signature, receive one count each.

Quarter-note rests.
Count, but do not play on the rests.

1   2   3   4   1   2   3   4

Eighth notes in 4/4 receive one half of a count.
Use the word "and" after each number.

Eighth-note rests

1 + 2 + 3 + 4 +   1 + 2 + 3 + 4 +

Sixteenth notes in 4/4 time receive one quarter of a count.
Use "e" after each number and "a" after each "and."

Sixteenth-note rests

1 e + a 2 e + a 3 e + a 4 e + a   1 e + a 2 e + a 3 e + a 4 e + a

Roll (multi bounces alternating between the right and left hands.)

R R L L R R L L

(32nd notes)

ANATOMY OF A DRUM BEAT

Music notation is nothing more than a representation of where a beat or count is located. Some of the beats are written as notes that we play on the drum, and others are written as rests that we count but don't play. It is the arrangement of these notes and rests that makes a song or rhythm come to life.

If you look at Example 1 on the next page, you will see four quarter notes played on the snare drum. In 4/4 time (sometimes called *common* time), there are four main beats or pulses. Quarter notes receive one beat or pulse each (think of four quarters to a dollar). Note the RLRL above the notes. These refer to your right and left hands. Counting out loud, slowly play the notes in the first example on the snare drum many times until you feel it is even and comfortable. Say "one, two, three, four" as you play. Keep your eyes focused on the music. Make sure that your taps on the snare are clean and single strokes. To accomplish this, make a slight effort to pick up the stick away from the head once you have struck the note with motion from your wrist. Example 2 shows the same notes on the same drum, but played with all right-hand strokes. Read and count this measure the same as the previous one. Once that feels good, do it again using all left-hand strokes.

It is now a simple matter to play the *ride* rhythm in Example 3 on a ride cymbal (usually a larger cymbal in the 18"–22" range) or on the closed hi-hat (use the left foot to press down on the pedal, thus closing the cymbals). Cymbals and sound effects like a cowbell or wood block are usually noted with "X's." Strike the cymbal about two or three inches from the edge closest to you. Still counting out loud, look at Example 4 and add the snare drum with your left hand on counts 2 and 4. Remember to keep the cymbal going, especially on counts 2 and 4.

It is time to add the bass drum with your right foot in Example 5 on beat 1. A good way to get into it is to start the right hand on the cymbal for a few measures, add the snare drum with the left hand on beats 2 and 4, and then when you are ready, tap the bass drum pedal on beat 1. To round out this rhythm, go to Example 6, which adds the bass drum to beat 3. Once you feel comfortable with this rhythm, gradually start playing it faster. If you play it too fast and can't control it, slow down and try it at a manageable tempo.

You've now covered the three main elements involved in a basic drumbeat: the kick drum, the snare drum, and a cymbal (hi-hat or ride). The remaining examples vary the patterns played on each instrument. Practice them slowly, and add the parts one at a time if needed until you're comfortable.

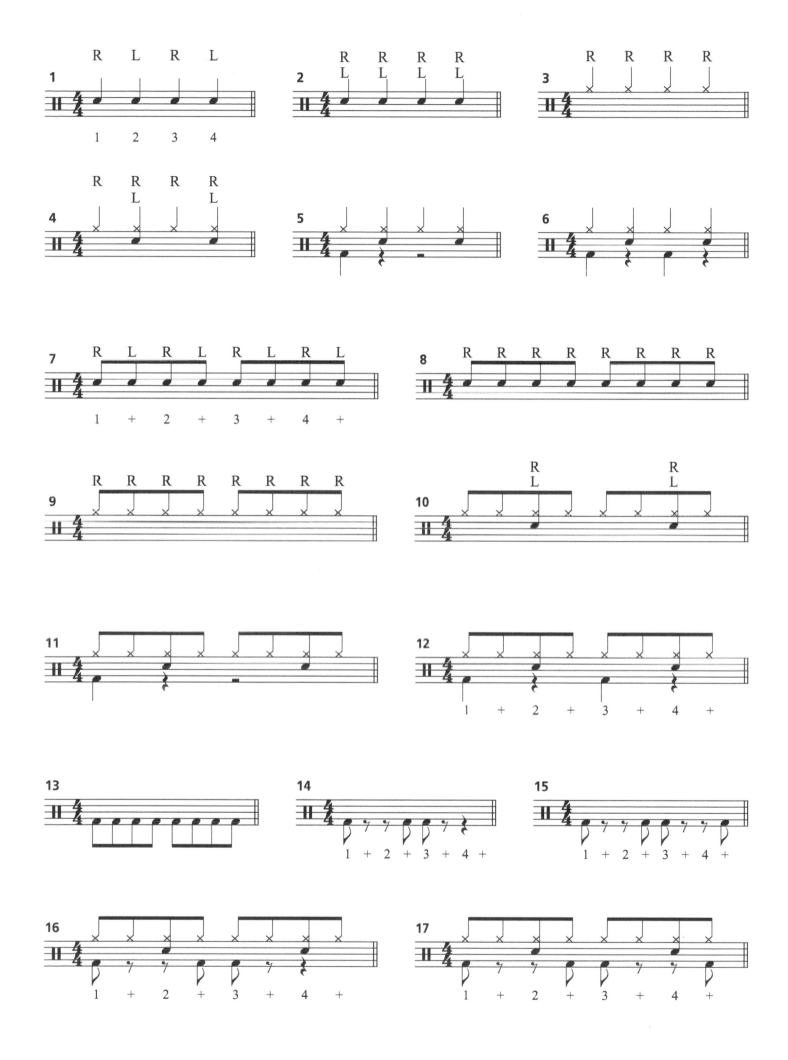

Lesson 2 • eighth-note Rock and Country Patterns

Once you get the basic eighth-note patterns in this section, it is merely a matter of changing the left hand to a *cross stick* position (also known as a *rim click, rim knock,* or *butt tap*) to give your sound a country flavor. For additional color, try the *right*-hand eighth-note pattern on the snare with a brush or rute. This will serve you well when backing up a vocal.

The cross stick is played by holding the *left* stick with the bead on the drum head and the butt of the stick edging over the rim at the 2:00 position. While holding the stick with the index finger and thumb, let the middle, ring, and pinkie fingers touch the drum head to deliver a dry "click." Don't lift the entire hand. Lift the stick by leaving the heel of the hand on the drum head while pivoting at the wrist. Position the butt end of the stick until you obtain a penetrating hollow *pop* similar to a wood block. Typically, about an inch or so over the rim should be adequate.

Variations and Fills

Earlier I wrote that music is built in phrases of two, four, and eight measures, and that *something* (especially on the fourth and eighth measures) needs to occur on the drums at these markers in the way of a variation to the rhythm. Example 5 shows how a single note added to the bass drum can change the whole feeling of the pattern. Examples 8–11 are fills or breaks that will help connect musical phrases. Try any of the rhythm patterns for one or three measures, and then drop in any of the fill patterns for more combinations.

Do's and Don'ts

    Do lock in with the bass player and create a rhythmic foundation for the group.

    Do not change the feel of the rhythm or color mid-phrase or on "odd" measures.

    Do not speed up or slow down on fills.

    Do not over-play variations. (Don't be accused of being a "busy" drummer.)

These patterns work great with the following songs:

"Ancient of Days"	"Lord I Lift Your Name on High"
"Awesome God"	"Shout to the Lord"
"Change My Heart Oh God"	"Secret Place"
"Hosanna"	"People Get Ready"
"In the Sanctuary"	"That's Why We Praise Him"
"I Will Celebrate"	"Without Him"
"Let the River Flow"	"Worthy, You Are Worthy"

LeSSON 3 · eiGhth-Note PATTERNS WITh OiSPLACeO LeFT haNO

The purpose of a displaced left hand is to change the traditional backbeat on counts 2 and 4, placing the stronger accent on an "and." This pattern really makes the music come alive from an unexpected direction. At first, playing these patterns may feel jarring and unsettling. Once you feel comfortable with the jaggedness of the rhythms, start putting together some two-measure patterns using a traditional eighth-note pattern for the first measure and a displaced pattern for the second measure, such as in Example 10. The beauty of these patterns is you can use them as an alternative fill at the end of a phrase, as well as a stand-alone rhythm pattern.

Do's and Don'ts
> **Do** practice slowly.
> **Do** experiment with different foot patterns.

These patterns work great with the following songs:

"Fuel"   "Open the Eyes of My Heart"
"I Walk By Faith"   "This Is the Day"
"Let It Rise"   "We Will Embrace Your Move"
"Lord, I Lift Your Name on High"   "We Bring the Sacrifice of Praise"
"My Redeemer Lives"

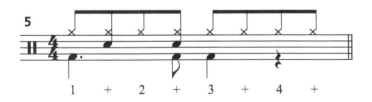

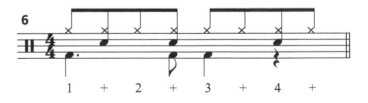

LESSON 4 • ROCK BALLAD WITH 16TH NOTES (RIGHT HAND)

When the music is soulful, slow, and eighth-note based, one way to give it some momentum is to play sixteenth notes on *top* of the closed hi-hat with the right hand.

For this pattern to be most effective, play the bass drum sparsely with a half-time feel. This half-time feel will create a strong foundation that will allow the vocalist or lead instrumentalist plenty of room to be expressive with his or her phrasing. For a different color, use the ride cymbal (lightly) for the sixteenth notes and add the hi-hat with the left foot on beats 2 and 4.

Another way to add color is to use a brush on the snare for the ride pattern. Playing the back beat with a cross stick on the snare is another effective way to back up a singer. Use the left stick directly on the drum head when the music opens up on a chorus.

Do's and Don'ts

Do play the hi-hat pattern with the bead of the stick, on *top* of the cymbal.

Do not play fast. These patterns are for slow to moderate tempos.

Do not get too busy on the fills.

Do not accent the hi-hat pattern.

These patterns work great with the following songs:

"Above All"
"Because He Lives"
"Breathe"
"Come Let Us Worship and Bow Down"
"Glorify Thy Name"
"Holy and Anointed One"
"In His Time"

"Jesus Draw Me Close"
"Jesus, Lover of My Soul"
"O How I Long"
"Redeemer Savior Friend"
"Take My Life"
"Think About His Love"

Slow to moderate tempo

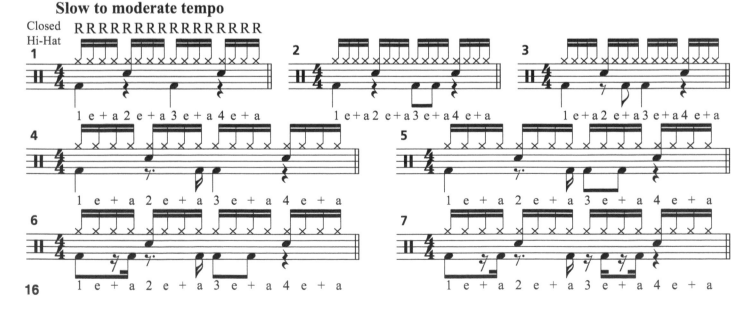

Lesson 5 • Rock Patterns with 16th Notes (both hands)

When the energy needs to increase, using sixteenths on the hi-hat with *both* hands is one popular way of heating up the music. Using both hands allows the music to be played faster. Care must be given to playing the sixteenth notes evenly, however, with no accents.

Playing sixteenth notes smoothly can be especially tricky when moving between the hi-hat and the snare drum. For color, using the shoulder of the sticks on the *edge* of the hi-hat creates a darker sound.

Because of the intensity of these patterns, it's easy to play too loudly; therefore, keep your sticks at a lower height.

Do's and Don'ts

Do use the bass drum judiciously.
Do not rush.

These patterns work great with the following songs:

"Come, Now Is the Time to Worship"　　　"Light the Fire Again"
"Hallelujah (Your Love Is Amazing)"　　　"Standing on the Rock"
"He's the Greatest"　　　　　　　　　　　"The River Is Here"
"I Will Not Forget You"　　　　　　　　　"Trading My Sorrows"
"In That Day"　　　　　　　　　　　　　"Worship You"

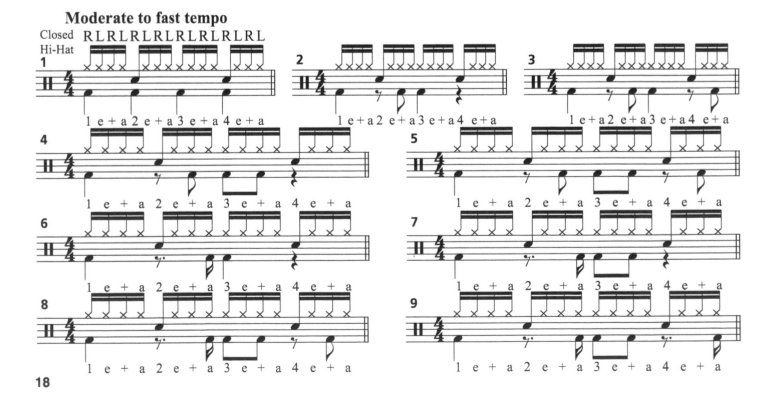

18

LESSON 6 • GOSPEL BALLAD WITH A TWELVE FEEL

Another way to be expressive at a slow tempo is to use 12/8 time. In 12/8 time, there are twelve beats in each measure, with every eighth note receiving one beat. Most of the time, however, composers will write a piece of music in 4/4 and insert the description: "twelve feel." This practice seems to bring out the triplet feel better than 12/8. Also, counting "1 and ah, 2 and ah, 3 and ah, 4 and ah" is easier to verbalize than "1 2 3, 4 5 6, 7 8 9, 10 11 12."

While learning patterns that include sixteenth notes (Examples 5, 6, 13, etc.) I find it useful to use a double count such as "one *and and* ah." If you turn the word "and" (in this case) into a two-syllable word *"eh-and,"* it will make the counting a bit easier. "A" becomes *"uh-uh,"* "one" becomes "wah-un," "two" becomes "too-oo," and so on.

This pattern works well with the right hand on the closed hi-hat or the ride cymbal. If you are using the ride cymbal, use the hi-hat with your left foot on counts 2 and 4. Using a cross stick on the snare is very effective underneath a vocal. Switch to the stick on the drum head when the music opens up. Some emphasis on counts 2 and 4 will help the music move along. Experiment using a fill as an introduction or pickup into the song. Typically this would be on beats 3 or 4 before the song starts. The leader will count off, for example, "1... 2..." and you might insert triplets on beats 3 and 4, which will bring the band in on the downbeat.

These patterns adapt easily for music written in 6/8 by just counting "1 and ah, 2 and ah" as shown in Examples 19 and 20.

Do's and Don'ts
> **Do** play slowly and deliberately.
> **Do** play the hi-hat on top of the cymbal with the bead of the stick.
> **Do** keep your fills in triplet form.
> **Do not** rush or drag on fills.

These patterns work great with the following songs:

"Beautiful Savior" (6/8)	"Jesus, Name Above All Names"
"Good to Me" (6/8)	"Soften My Heart"
"Great Is the Lord"	"We Will Dance"
"He Is Exalted"	"When We See Him"

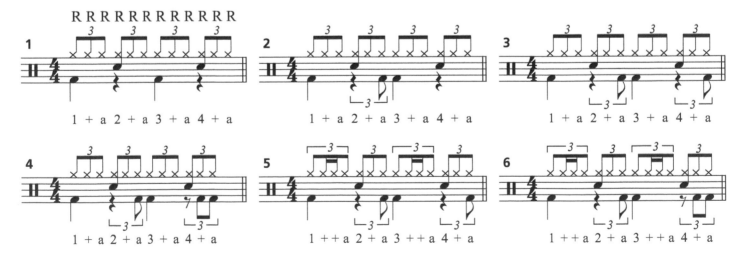

LESSON 7 • SWING PATTERNS

Start the swing pattern by playing triplets on the ride cymbal with a 12 feel in Example 1. Trim the triplets back to quarter notes on counts 1 and 3 (Example 2), and then trim the middle note of the triplet after counts 2 and 4 (Example 3). Example 4 represents an alternative way of writing Example 3. Finally, add the left foot on the hi-hat on beats 2 and 4 (Example 5). The ride pattern should be laid back and sound like: "chang, chang'a lang, chang'a lang."

When adding the left foot on the hi-hat, it is very effective to "rock" the foot forward to close the cymbals. While the toes push down on the pedal, lift the heel up to create the familiar "chick" sound from the cymbals. The added pressure from this ankle move ensures that the cymbals close all the way. When the cymbals don't close tightly, the chick sound is lost, and you create a crash sound, which at this point is inappropriate.

These exercises require independent limb coordination and are not always easy to grasp the first time. Practice very slowly with hands only, and then add feet. Your patience will be rewarded with a relaxed swinging style. Unlike other styles, in the swing style it is generally okay to change the right-hand ride patterns from measure to measure. The four-measure pattern (Example 13) keeps the feet and the left hand the same, while the ride pattern in the right hand changes. Just remember to return to the basic swing pattern (Example 5).

When playing triplet fills, you might find it useful to use a transitional note with the left hand on the snare on count "ah" of beat 3 (Example 14). This gives the right hand a chance to get off the cymbal and onto a drum for the fill. Can the ride patterns be played on the high-hat? Sure! You can play on the hi-hat in either of two ways. One way is to keep the cymbals closed for the entire pattern, playing on top of the cymbal lightly. This sound is good for softer passages or under a vocalist. A second and more traditional way is to keep the left foot opening the hi-hat on counts 1 and 3 (closing on counts 2 and 4) while continuing a ride pattern. This adds a splash of sound, is still relatively soft in volume, and adds a decisive accent on the 2 and 4 when the hi-hat closes.

Do's and Don'ts
> **Do** play patterns with a relaxed triplet feel.
> **Do not** play ride patterns stiffly.
> **Do not** play the bass drum with a heavy foot.

These patterns work great with the following songs:
> "God Is Good All the Time"
> "I've Got Peace Like a River"
> "Joshua Fit the Battle of Jericho"
> "Just a Closer Walk with Thee"

> "One More Battle to Fight"
> "Swing Low Sweet Chariot"
> "When the Saints Come Marching In"

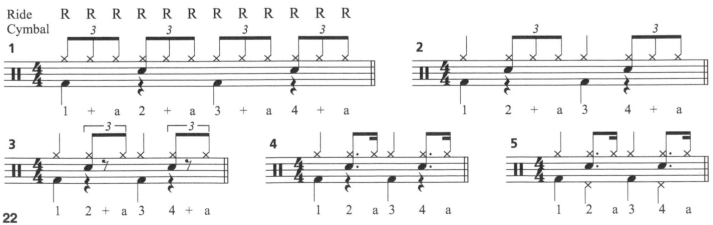

Ride Variations

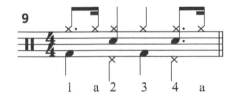

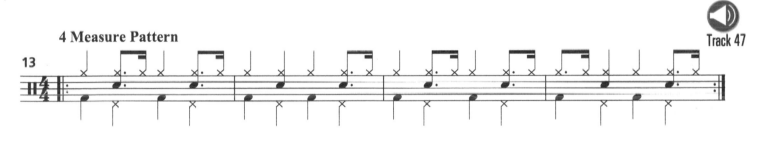

2 Measure Pattern

Track 46

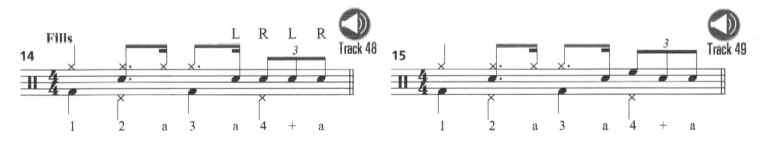

4 Measure Pattern

Track 47

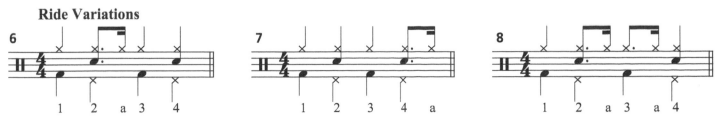

Fills

Track 48
Track 49
Track 50
Track 51

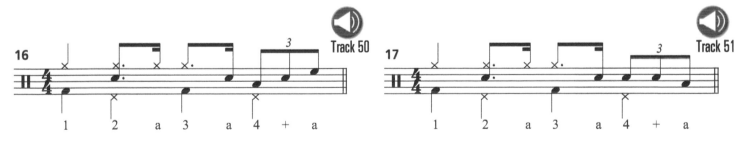

4 Measure Pattern with Fill

Track 52

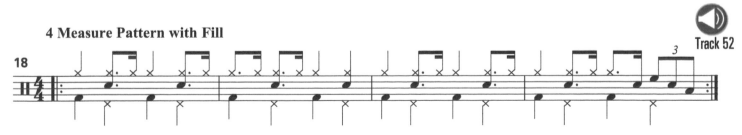

LeSSON 8 · shuffle PATTerNS

The shuffle is an old-timey music form with its roots in early gospel and spirituals. Example 1 shows a 12-feel pattern from which to start. Similar to the swing pattern, you leave out the middle eighth note ("and"). Unlike the swing pattern, you leave the note out for *every* triplet group, resulting in a *jumpy* count of "1-ah, 2-ah, 3-ah, 4-ah" (Example 2). Example 3 demonstrates another common way to write this rhythm. If one uses the word *merrily* to get the feel of a triplet, the shuffle will sound like "*mer - ly, mer - ly, mer - ly, mer - ly.*" The color possibilities include using a closed hi-hat and cross stick, closed hi-hat and snare drum, and ride cymbal and snare drum. When you use the ride cymbal, try using the hi-hat with your left foot on beats 2 and 4. To help your right hand get to the fills in time, it is a good technique to launch off the left hand. Examples 14 and 15 demonstrate this launching note on the "a" of beat 2. Examples 16 and 17 have the launching note on the same count, but have two sixteenth notes (double counted as "a, a").

Patterns 18 and 19 use what is called a *quarter-note triplet* for the fill. I chose to write it out in eighth notes, which is a bit easier to understand for newer drummers. Essentially, every *other* note of the triplet is played. Play these with the right hand and accent very deliberately. To feel the quarter-note triplet better, try tapping triplets by alternating your hands on your lap (start with the right hand) and slowly lift the left hand off your lap while keeping the left hand in motion. What you'll have remaining is your right hand playing quarter-note triplets.

Do's and Don'ts

Do play with momentum and ahead of the beat if playing at quicker tempo.
Do play just behind the beat and relaxed if playing at slower tempo.
Do not rush.
Do not play as an eighth-note rock pattern.

These patterns work great with the following songs:

"Closet Religion"   "Let Us Break Bread Together"
"Joshua Fit the Battle of Jericho"   "You Are God"

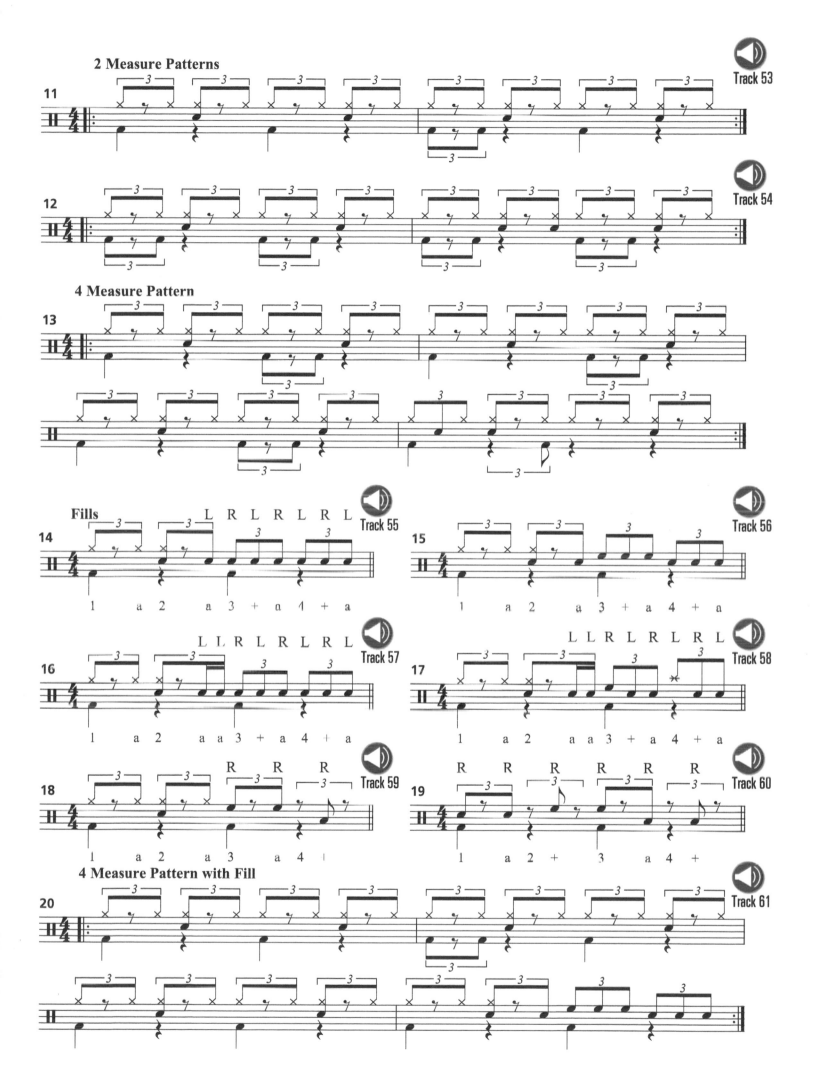

Lesson 9 • The Gospel Two Step

This pattern is used extensively where there is a need for a fast pulse with a strong back beat. Examples 1–3 are written in 4/4 time for clarity, but we change to 2/4 time with Example 4. Using a closed hi-hat played with the stick on the top of the cymbal is a popular way to play this pattern. When the music gets enthusiastic, the player can use a ride cymbal. Using the ride cymbal lets the left foot be employed on the hi-hat as shown in Example 5.

Examples 6–8 use sixteenth notes on the snare drum. They should all be played with the left hand. Example 9 is a country style two-step with beats 1 and 2 on the ride cymbal. This is an interesting alternate pattern that can also be played with brushes or rute on the snare drum. Be sure to accent the counts "e and." The effect can conjure up the feel of a train rolling down the tracks. All fills here are one measure breaks.

Do's and Don'ts
> **Do** play *on* the beat with precision.
> **Do not** rush.

These patterns work great with the following songs:
> "Come Into His Presence"   "Send a Revival"
> "God Is Good All the Time"   "Will the Circle Be Unbroken"
> "I Saw the Light"   "We Are Marching Home"
> "I'm Going Through Jesus"   "Lean on the Everlasting Arms"
> "I've Got Peace Like a River"

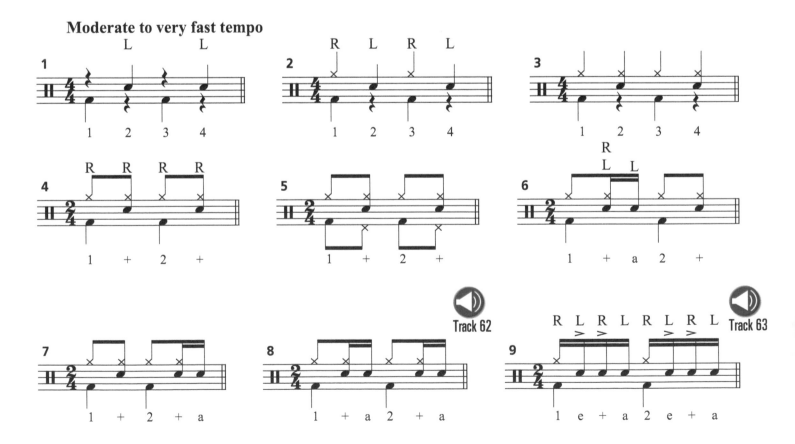

LESSON 10 • 3/4 WALTZ

Included in this section are three types of waltzes. They are the traditional waltz, the swing waltz, and the country waltz. Generally, waltzes are played lightly, at low volume, and with precision. It is easy to rush a waltz, and great care must be taken to keep the pulse in time. The drummer can do this by counting "one and two and three and." Adding the "and" to the count helps regulate the time.

In a traditional waltz (Examples 1–4) and a swing waltz (Examples 5–11), most often the ride cymbal is employed. This allows the left foot to be used on the hi-hat on beats 2 and 3. The country waltz can use a closed hi-hat (played on top) and cross stick, as well as a ride cymbal, with the stick hitting the drum head. Using a brush or rute on the snare drum in place of the cymbal creates a nice timbre.

The first two-measure pattern (Example 15) can be used as a traditional waltz *or* mild swing waltz. Example 16 is a two-measure country pattern. Example 17 is a four-measure swing pattern, while Example 18 is a four-measure country waltz pattern.

Do's and Don'ts

    Do play fills judiciously and cleanly.

    Do not overplay the bass drum.

These patterns work great with the following songs:

"Amazing Grace"
"Come Thou Fount of Every Blessing"
"Lamb of God"
"Lambs in the Valley"
"Morning Has Broken"

"No More Night"
"The Old Rugged Cross"
"Open Our Eyes"
"Silent Night"

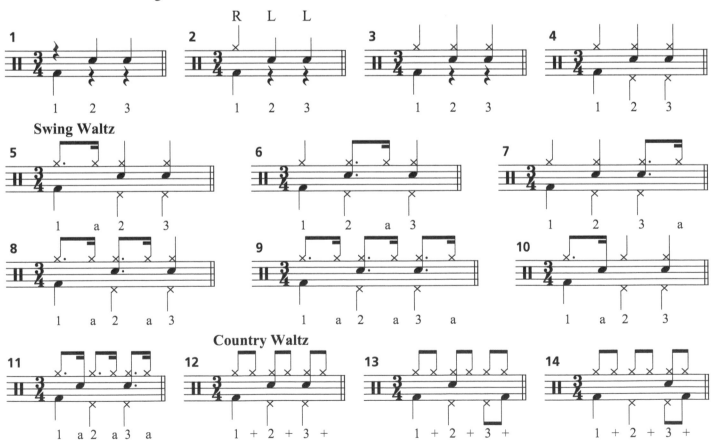

2 Measure Patterns

15   Track 71

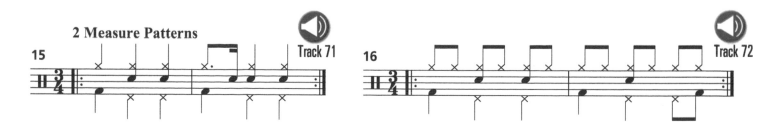

16   Track 72

4 Measure Patterns

17   Track 73

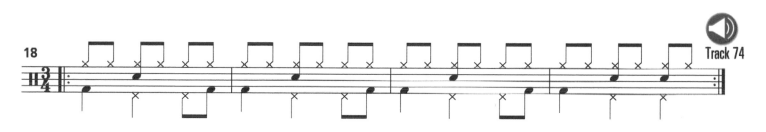

18   Track 74

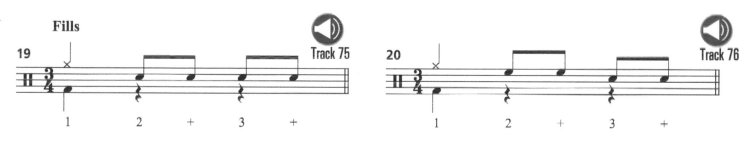

Fills

19   Track 75

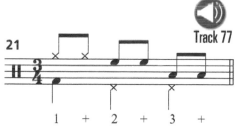

1   2   +   3   +

20   Track 76

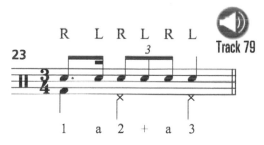

1   2   +   3   +

21   Track 77

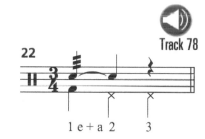

1   +   2   +   3   +

22   Track 78

1 e + a 2   3

R   L   R   L   R   L

23   Track 79

1   a   2   +   a   3

4 Measure Patterns with Fill

24   Track 80

25   Track 81

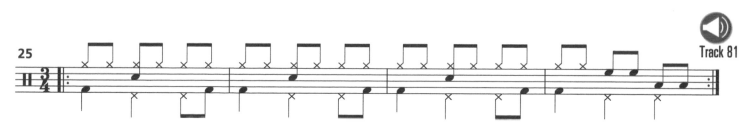

Lesson 11 • World Rhythms

Knowing some world rhythms can be very useful for the drummer, not only at Sunday services, but at holiday pageants as well. In depicting ancient times and the life of biblical figures, a well placed Middle Eastern or Moorish rhythm can be exactly what is needed to bring a part of the service to life. Culturally authentic instruments such as the *dumbek, bendir, daf, tar,* and *riq* can all be used, as well as modern congas, bongos, and tambourine. While the following patterns are scored for drumset, they can easily be transferred to hand drums.

All rhythms are to be played with snares *off*. Use cymbals very lightly if at all. In Examples 1–5, a cross stick for all left-handed strokes adds a nice pop to the rhythms. The Cuban Bolero in Examples 6–7 is to be played at a very slow tempo. Example 7 has an unusual sticking, which can be used with a cross stick in the left hand. The Bolero can also be a good ad-libbed rhythm on the hi-hat when castanets are called for. The Calypso patterns in Examples 10–11 are written in 2/4 and are not to be played too quickly. The syncopation in the foot is a bit awkward until you get used to it. You might work up to it by just playing the bass drum on beats 1 and 2. Calypsos are played very lightly. You can combine Examples 10 and 11 for a two-measure pattern.

Whereas the Ayub (Example 12) could be played with two lefts on the sixteenth notes, I have written the sticking in a way that seems to bring out the accent on the upbeats better. The Sayyidii in Example 17 includes a five-stroke roll. This roll should end on the first note of the next measure. Combining Examples 16 and 17 makes for a good two-measure pattern. The Nawarji pattern (Example 18) is a slow to moderate rhythm. Use a cross stick only on the last two lefts.

Do's and Don'ts

Do try these patterns with hands (no sticks) on your drum set.

These patterns work great with the following songs:

"He Knows My Name"   "Victory Chant" (Calypso or Ayub)
(Rhumba, Ayub, or Bolero)   "Mary's Little Boy Child" (Calypso)
"Mighty Is Our God" (Calypso or Rhumba)   "Oh Magnify the Lord" (Calypso)

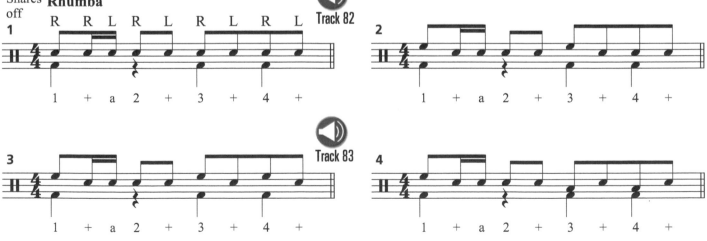

LESSON 12 • MARCHES

Now and then, the drummer is called on to march a group of people into or out of the sanctuary. In the following examples you will find two marches in 4/4 and one in 6/8. The hi-hat part is best played by bouncing the cymbals off each other to simulate the sound of hand-held crash cymbals. The best way to get this marching band effect is to anchor the heel of the left foot on the heel plate of the high-hat stand. Keeping the foot stiff, tap down on the pedal with the ball of the foot and toes. The two-measure "Roll Off" is a traditional cue to bring a military band into a march. The drummer may use it to start the group marching or, as intended, to cue the band into the beginning of a musical selection.

These patterns work great as intros to the songs:
"Onward Christian Soldiers" (4/4)
"March of the Toy Soldiers" (6/8)

Track 93

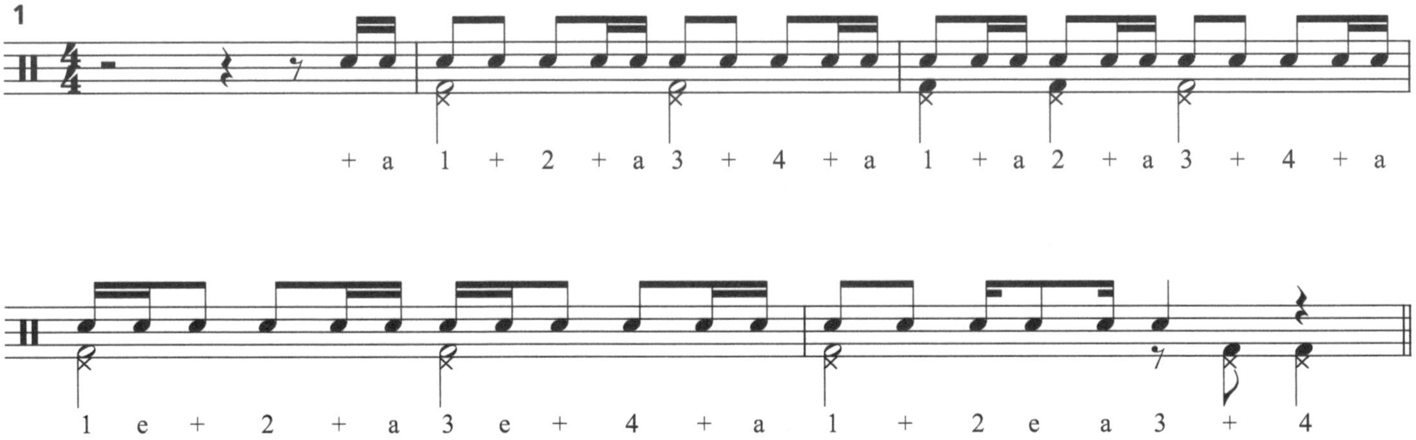

Track 94

Lesson 13 • brushes/rutes

It is important to realize that brushes are played with an entirely different approach than that of sticks. Example 1 shows the clockwise path for a left-hand *sweep*. Starting near the top for beat 1, the brush rotates down for beat 2, back up again where the brush started for beat 3, and then down to beat 4, and so on. Keeping the brush at an angle uses the tips of the wires and produces the "white noise" that fills the space in slow tunes. It is vital to keep the sweep *round* as opposed to oval-shaped. In a matched grip, the bristles will most likely be facing upwards as it travels. With a *traditional* grip the bristles face to the right, which lends itself a bit better to the sweep shown in Example 2. This sweep is a gentle pressing (flattening) of the wires *onto* the head, adding a subtle pulse on beats 2 and 4. The drummer takes the pressure off the brush (going back on the tips of the bristles) when returning to beats 1 or 3. Keeping the circle round, while at the same time sweeping on the upbeats, will take much practice.

To add rhythm, try tapping quarter notes with the tips of the *right* brush on beats 1, 2, 3, and 4. While tapping the right brush you must keep the circle going with the *left* brush at the same time. Avoid contact by either brush by moving the right brush from right to left and back again in a fairly straight line (Example 3). The right brush does *not* sweep but merely lifts and taps at the points shown in the example. For *medium* and *up* tempos, it is then a simple matter to add a triplet feel with the right hand by adding the "ah" after beats 2 and 4 (Example 4). In this way the drummer's hands work together to create the "swish" sound while at the same time supplying the familiar "tick, ticka, tick, ticka" rhythm used in swing rhythms.

As if brushwork were not already a coordination challenge, now add the hi-hat on beats 2 and 4 with the left foot! Example 5 shows the left-hand sweep for a waltz in 3/4. Syncopated accents on counts "e" and "a" can be handled with the left hand. This is accomplished by lifting the brush and sharply rapping the flat side of the wires into the head creating a *slap*. The experienced brush handler does all this while keeping the sweep going with the left and the ride rhythm with the right. This is not an easy task. Cymbal playing with brushes can be very frustrating since the sound barely projects beyond the drums. In an odd turn-around, the precursor of the brush, called the *Rute*, has made its way back into the modern percussion section and is ideal for soft yet audible cymbal articulation. The bundle of dowels that makes up the modern day rute is a bit louder than a brush and retains the bounce and control of a stick. While not great for left hand sweeps, it *is* a lifesaver in the *right* hand for cymbals. As of this printing, Vic Firth makes three models of wooden doweled rutes, as well as two nylon bristled models.

brush patterns

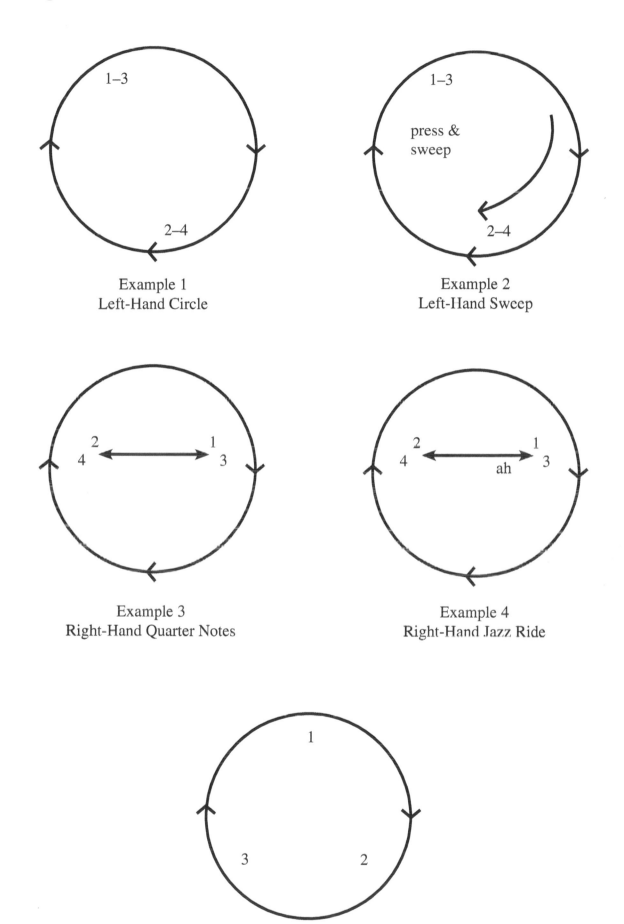

Example 1
Left-Hand Circle

Example 2
Left-Hand Sweep

Example 3
Right-Hand Quarter Notes

Example 4
Right-Hand Jazz Ride

Example 5
Left-Hand Sweep in 3/4

LESSON 14 • FREE TIME

Playing in free time is an art and probably better experienced than written about; however, you can use these comments as a jumping off place for your own style. There are times when a vocalist may start a verse *before* the band comes in to set the rhythm. Often at this time, the keyboard or guitar may back the singer from underneath with chords played slowly, softly, and without a pulse. Another free time moment may occur before the offertory. Similarly, the organist, pianist, or guitarist might play melody or chords with the pulse missing. At these opportunities, the drummer is best advised to stay low and out of the way. One way to contribute, however, is by producing cymbal scrapes. Scrapes are done on top of a ride cymbal with an ordinary coin. With the coin's edge, lightly scrape the cymbal from the dome to the edge. This can be done with a slow or quick motion, depending on the effect you want. The metal pull rod of a brush works just as well. Using mallets or rutes for soft rolls on cymbals is another way to achieve color in a free time interlude. Shakers and windchimes are two other musical textures that can be used.

Exactly *when* to come in with these effects is left to the drummer's discretion. There is no downbeat. Generally the count is stretched out. The drummer is best advised to use taste and jump in when it feels right. Listen and watch for cues, as at some point, a steady rhythm has to be set if the tune is to continue. A short fill or a well-placed rim shot may be all that is needed to get the song (rhythmically) in gear. Sometimes a whispered count-in, or a time count clicked on the sticks to the rest of the ensemble is all that is necessary. This is accomplished as the singer is holding onto the last note of the phrase, with you counting, "one... two... one-two-three-four" (assuming the music is in 4/4).

Examples of free time are found in the songs:
> "Change My Heart Oh God"
> "Give Thanks"
> "I Need You Now"
> "More Precious than Silver"
> "O How I Long"

appendix

The following is a list of songs and the patterns that would be appropriate for each.

Eighth-Note Rock Patterns
"Ancient of Days," "Awesome God," "Change My Heart Oh God," "Hosanna," "In the Sanctuary," "I Will Celebrate," "Let the River Flow," "Lord I Lift Your Name on High," "Shout to the Lord," "Secret Place," "People Get Ready," "That's Why We Praise Him," "Without Him," "Worthy, You Are Worthy."

Eighth-Note Patterns with Displaced Left Hand
"Fuel," "I Walk By Faith," "Let It Rise," "Lord, I Lift Your Name on High," "My Redeemer Lives," "Open the Eyes of My Heart," "This Is the Day," "We Will Embrace Your Move," "We Bring the Sacrifice of Praise."

Rock Ballad with 16th Notes
"Above All," "Because He Lives," "Breathe," "Come Let Us Worship and Bow Down," "Glorify Thy Name," "Holy and Anointed One," "In His Time," "Jesus Draw Me Close," "Jesus, Lover of My Soul," "O How I Long," "Redeemer Savior Friend," "Take My Life," "Think About His Love."

16th Note Patterns with Both Hands
"Come, Now Is the Time to Worship," "Hallelujah (Your Love Is Amazing)," "He's the Greatest," "I Will Not Forget You," "In That Day," "Light the Fire Again," "Standing on the Rock," "The River Is Here," "Trading My Sorrows," "Worship You."

Gospel Ballad with a 12 Feel
"Beautiful Savior" (6/8), "Good to Me" (6/8), "Great Is the Lord," "He Is Exalted," "Jesus, Name Above All Names," "Soften My Heart," "We Will Dance," "When We See Him."

Swing Patterns
"God Is Good All the Time," "I've Got Peace Like a River," "Joshua Fit the Battle of Jericho," "Just a Closer Walk with Thee," "One More Battle to Fight," "Swing Low Sweet Chariot," "When the Saints Come Marching In."

Shuffle Patterns
"Closet Religion," "Joshua Fit the Battle of Jericho," "Let Us Break Bread Together," "You Are God."

Gospel Two Step
"Come Into His Presence," "God Is Good All the Time," "I Saw the Light," "I'm Going Through Jesus," "I've Got Peace Like a River," "Send a Revival," "Will the Circle Be Unbroken," "We Are Marching Home," "Lean on the Everlasting Arms."

3/4 Waltz
"Amazing Grace," "Come Thou Fount of Every Blessing," "Lamb of God," "Lambs in the Valley," "Morning Has Broken," "No More Night," "The Old Rugged Cross," "Open Our Eyes," "Silent Night."

World Rhythms

"He Knows My Name" (Rhumba, Ayub, or Bolero), "Mighty Is Our God" (Calypso or Rhumba), "Victory Chant" (Calypso or Ayub), "Mary's Little Boy Child" (Calypso), "Oh Magnify the Lord" (Calypso).

Marches

Intro to "Onward Christian Soldiers" (4/4), intro to "March of the Toy Soldiers" (6/8).

Free Time

"Change My Heart Oh God," "Give Thanks," "I Need You Now," "More Precious than Silver," "O How I Long."

aBOUT ThE AUThOR

Cary Nasatir is the director of the Nasatir School of Percussion, a private teaching facility in Castro Valley, California. In addition to the school, Cary is an adjunct faculty member at Patten Christian University in Oakland, CA, a percussion clinician for the Ludwig Drum Company, percussion staff advisor to three San Francisco Bay Area schools, and has published several articles on percussion for various national music magazines. Nasatir studied percussion in his hometown of Chicago with Roy C. Knapp, Jose Bethancourt, Casper Boghosian, Haskell W. Harr, and Donald Knapp, as well as conducting with Manuel Piculas. He is a graduate of Columbia College, Chicago.

Cary's Website is: **http://www.nsopdrums.com**

Cary is endorsed by Vic Firth Sticks, Sabian Cymbals, Aquarian Drumheads, and Rhythm Tech Percussion.

YOU CAN'T BEAT OUR DRUM BOOKS!

Bass Drum Control
Best Seller for More Than 50 Years!
by Colin Bailey
This perennial favorite among drummers helps players develop their bass drum technique and increase their flexibility through the mastery of exercises.
06620020 Book/Online Audio $17.99

The Complete Drumset Rudiments
by Peter Magadini
Use your imagination to incorporate these rudimental etudes into new patterns that you can apply to the drumset or tom toms as you develop your hand technique with the Snare Drum Rudiments, your hand and foot technique with the Drumset Rudiments and your polyrhythmic technique with the Polyrhythm Rudiments. Adopt them all into your own creative expressions based on ideas you come up with while practicing.
06620016 Book/CD Pack $14.95

Drum Aerobics
by Andy Ziker
A 52-week, one-exercise-per-day workout program for developing, improving, and maintaining drum technique. Players of all levels – beginners to advanced – will increase their speed, coordination, dexterity and accuracy. The online audio contains all 365 workout licks, plus play-along grooves in styles including rock, blues, jazz, heavy metal, reggae, funk, calypso, bossa nova, march, mambo, New Orleans 2nd Line, and lots more!
06620137 Book/Online Audio $19.99

Drumming the Easy Way!
The Beginner's Guide to Playing Drums for Students and Teachers
by Tom Hapke
Cherry Lane Music
Now with online audio! This book takes the beginning drummer through the paces – from reading simple exercises to playing great grooves and fills. Each lesson includes a preparatory exercise and a solo. Concepts and rhythms are introduced one at a time, so growth is natural and easy. Features large, clear musical print, intensive treatment of each individual drum figure, solos following each exercise to motivate students, and more!
02500876 Book/Online Audio..$19.99
02500191 Book...$14.99

The Drumset Musician – 2nd Edition
by Rod Morgenstein and Rick Mattingly
Containing hundreds of practical, usable beats and fills, *The Drumset Musician* teaches you how to apply a variety of patterns and grooves to the actual performance of songs. The accompanying online audio includes demos as well as 18 play-along tracks covering a wide range of rock, blues and pop styles, with detailed instructions on how to create exciting, solid drum parts.
00268369 Book/Online Audio..............................$19.99

HAL•LEONARD®
www.halleonard.com

Prices, contents, and availability subject to change without notice.

Instant Guide to Drum Grooves
The Essential Reference for the Working Drummer
by Maria Martinez
Become a more versatile drumset player! From traditional Dixieland to cutting-edge hip-hop, *Instant Guide to Drum Grooves* is a handy source featuring 100 patterns that will prepare working drummers for the stylistic variety of modern gigs. The book includes essential beats and grooves in such styles as: jazz, shuffle, country, rock, funk, New Orleans, reggae, calypso, Brazilian and Latin.
06620056 Book/CD Pack $12.99

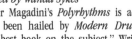

1001 Drum Grooves
The Complete Resource for Every Drummer
by Steve Mansfield
Cherry Lane Music
This book presents 1,001 drumset beats played in a variety of musical styles, past and present. It's ideal for beginners seeking a well-organized, easy-to-follow encyclopedia of drum grooves, as well as consummate professionals who want to bring their knowledge of various drum styles to new heights. Author Steve Mansfield presents: rock and funk grooves, blues and jazz grooves, ethnic grooves, Afro-Cuban and Caribbean grooves, and much more.

02500337 Book...$14.99

Polyrhythms – The Musician's Guide
by Peter Magadini
edited by Wanda Sykes
Peter Magadini's *Polyrhythms* is acclaimed the world over and has been hailed by *Modern Drummer* magazine as "by far the best book on the subject." Written for instrumentalists and vocalists alike, this book with online audio contains excellent solos and exercises that feature polyrhythmic concepts. Topics covered include: 6 over 4, 5 over 4, 7 over 4, 3 over 4, 11 over 4, and other rhythmic ratios; combining various polyrhythms; polyrhythmic time signatures; and much more. The audio includes demos of the exercises and is accessed online using the unique code in each book.
06620053 Book/Online Audio...$19.99

Joe Porcaro's Drumset Method – Groovin' with Rudiments
Patterns Applied to Rock, Jazz & Latin Drumset
by Joe Porcaro
Master teacher Joe Porcaro presents rudiments at the drumset in this sensational new edition of *Groovin' with Rudiments*. This book is chock full of exciting drum grooves, sticking patterns, fills, polyrhythmic adaptations, odd meters, and fantastic solo ideas in jazz, rock, and Latin feels. The online audio features 99 audio clip examples in many styles to round out this true collection of superb drumming material for every serious drumset performer.
06620129 Book/Online Audio $24.99

66 Drum Solos for the Modern Drummer
Rock • Funk • Blues • Fusion • Jazz
by Tom Hapke
Cherry Lane Music
66 Drum Solos for the Modern Drummer presents drum solos in all styles of music in an easy-to-read format. These solos are designed to help improve your technique, independence, improvisational skills, and reading ability on the drums and at the same time provide you with some cool licks that you can use right away in your own playing.
02500319 Book/Online Audio...$17.99